# INFERNAL DEVICE

disinformation®

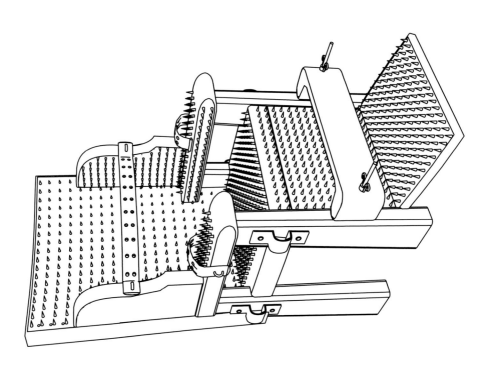

# INFERNAL DEVICE

## the machinery of torture and execution

### ERIK C. RÜHLING

© 2007 Erik Rühling

Published by The Disinformation Company Ltd.
163 Third Avenue, Suite 108
New York, NY 10003
Tel.: +1.212.691.1605 Fax: +1.212.691.1606 www.disinfo.com

The models in this book were created in Alias (now Autodesk) Maya and rendered using Illuminate Labs' Turtle.

Titles and headings set in FF Disturbance, body set in Franklin Gothic Book.

Design & Layout: Erik Rühling

Library of Congress Control Number: 2007932100

ISBN-13: 978-1-932857-89-4

Printed in Thailand

10 9 8 7 6 5 4 3 2 1

Distributed in the USA and Canada by Consortium Book Sales and Distribution
Tel.: +1.651.221.9035 Fax: +1.651.221.0124 www.cbsd.com
Distributed in the United Kingdom and Eire by Virgin Books
Tel.: +44.(0)20.7386.3300 Fax: +44.(0)20.7386.3360 E-Mail: sales@virgin-books.co.uk
Distributed in Australia by Tower Books
Tel.: +61.2.9975.5566 Fax: +61.2.9975.5599 Email: info@towerbooks.com.au

Attention colleges and universities, corporations and other organizations: Quantity discounts are available on bulk purchases of this book for educational training purposes, fund-raising, or gift giving. Special books, booklets, or book excerpts can also be created to fit your specific needs. For information contact the Marketing Department of The Disinformation Company Ltd.

Disinformation is a registered trademark of The Disinformation Company Ltd.

"pity this busy monster, manunkind..."

— e.e. cummings

# table of contents

# acknowledgments

I would like to acknowledge the invaluable assistance and support, in words and deeds, given to me by my family and friends during the creation of this book. A great deal of thanks is also extended to the many visitors to the website who offered suggestions, criticisms, and sometimes simply thoughtful correspondence throughout this project. There's a surprising number of people out there in the world interested in this subject. I promise not to reveal your names.

*You know who you are.*

# Preface

I began collecting information about the devices in this book over ten years ago with the intention of creating a book that presented them to the reader in a visual style that was more accessible and descriptive than the various museum photographs, line art drawings, woodcuts, or verbal explanations that had been duplicated throughout most of the accessible research materials. It seemed as if once there was a halfway decent drawing or photograph of a particular device that it was forever destined to reproduce itself, virus-like, throughout the literature. These devices were in dire need of new visual representations.

The easiest way, it seemed, for me to recreate these contraptions would be to construct them in a virtual space. In this way, the items could be rendered from any view, capturing the essence of the machinery in a way that woodcuts and drawings cannot. To that end, I taught myself how to use a 3D software package, gathered up my best drawings and photos, and set out modeling and rendering as many machines of torture and execution as I could find. This resulted in the database found at www.occasionalhell.com/infdevice.

Over the years, this database has proved to be immensely popular and renderings have been used in such wildly diverse publications as a book on Polish law to an article in *Maxim* magazine. I again picked up the original vision of a printed work, considering that this was a subject in which many people were guiltily interested, like the rubberneckers at a car wreck.

Three years later, here are what I consider the best and most interesting of the results—a menagerie of machines that are both cruel and unusual.

# INTRODUCTION

Any history of humanity must include a history of humanity's machines. From the first stick used to dig roots out of the ground to the most complex of atomic particle accelerators, the story of humanity is the story of humanity's machines. Humanity's history of course, has taken its fair share of dark turns. Wars, slavery, genocide, torture—these are the idiomatic skeletons in humanity's closet, displaying, if nothing else, the dual nature of mankind. It is no surprise, then, that man has invented and repurposed both new and old tools and machines in pursuit of these darker labors.

The machines in these pages range from the dreadfully simple (the chain scourge), to the needlessly elaborate (the brazen bull), but they all have been invented exclusively to cause physical or mental pain, or, in some cases, to end life. There are plain, austere devices born of immediate necessity, like the torture shears, and there are extravagant works of art, like the branks, that display a technical skill and attention to detail that belie the true purpose of the device. There are screws, levers, pulleys, wheels, and axles—all pressed into the service of torture and execution.

Each device is presented herein with a short description and one or more three-dimensional renderings. Information has come from both first- and second-hand accounts, drawings, and photographs. In some cases, the legend associated with a particular device may have overstepped the facts, and where appropriate, this is noted—however, this should not detract from the curiosity of the object, as sometimes the myth tells more about the minds of men than the truth.

In ancient Greek drama, a Latin phrase was used to describe a divine being emerging from a highly-wrought machine, indubitably to eliminate catastrophe, tie up loose ends, and bring the play to a close. This phrase was *"deus ex machina,"* or "god from the machine," as the benevolent spirit arose from the plot mechanism. The machines in this book, however, lack any hint of the divine, and if anything are imbued with the dark urges of humanity. If properly named, they would be declared *"infernus ex machina,"*—hell from the machine.

# I. PUNISHMENTS VILE

*"Let the punishment match the offense."*

—*Cicero*

# BARReL PiLLORy

The town ne'er-do-well would have been familiar with the embrace of this portable instrument of torture, known variously as the "barrel pillory," the "drunkard's cloak," or the "Spanish[1] mantle." This pillory was often reserved for those disposed to excessive drinking, and what better object to use than the barrel which may have previously contained similar spirits which led to the accused's undoing. Imagine the town drunk, perhaps in the throes of a raging hangover, forced into the confines of a cumbersome oaken cask, fermenting with latter-day tipple and present-day bodily excretions. Not an enjoyable way to spend the day, to say the least.

Like the more recognizable stationary pillory or "stocks" (ubiquitous among re-creations of old-country and colonial villages), the purpose of the barrel pillory was to subject the unlucky occupants to torment by their peers. Along with verbal epithets, the tormentors also hurled solid objects, generally rotten, at the victim's head. Rotted vegetables were always popular, along with manure (animal and human), and small rocks.

The device was constructed like this—a large barrel fit over the entire body, with the unfortunate occupant's head poking out from the hole in the top like a "mantle," a sleeveless robe worn by the clergy. From there, the pillory could take alternate forms—an enclosed barrel forced the victim to stand in place for hours (most likely in the heat of the town square), while an open barrel with holes for the arms and an open bottom allowed the victim to roam about town. An example of the stationary barrel, specifically named "the Spanish mantle" sported an enclosure for the head made of small iron bars, much like a catcher's mitt. Presumably this was for the safety of

---

1   The Spanish really got the short end of the stick when it came to the naming of torture devices, as we shall see. It may have been that whole "Inquisition" thing.

A barrel pillory with a starburst shaped collar.
Should the occupant fall over, the head is protected
and the barrel will not roll, demonstrating that even
in a torture device there is room for safety.

the occupant, although it was just as likely a way to ensure he or she would not be knocked unconscious, a catastrophe which would have robbed the townspeople of their entertainment. A version in Berlin measured 1' 8" diameter at the top, 2' 11" diameter at the bottom, and 2' 11" tall, no doubt being an example of the ambulatory model (our ancestors being shorter, but not that much shorter).

If a town was in possession of an "official" barrel pillory, there may have been scenes painted on the side of the barrel depicting the transgressions of which the victim was accused. Public drunkenness, brawling, petty theft, and scandalous romancing were popular themes, all punishable offenses in those days, but just another typical evening at, say, Mardi Gras in New Orleans.

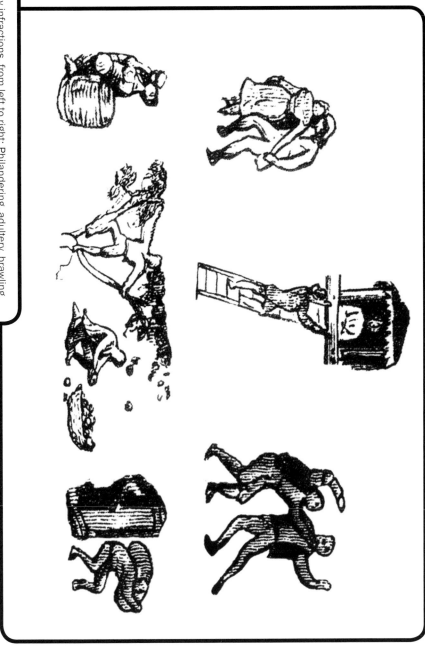

Blameworthy infractions, from left to right: Philandering, adultery, brawling, drinking, theft, and robbery. Adapted from Held 1985, fig. 56.

# BeLL coLLaR

A subtle yet insidious form of torture, the bell collar was valued for the fact that it allowed wardens to keep tabs on their prisoners while tormenting them with the ringing of a bell hung just above the head.

The suffering meted out by this instrument was not physical, but rather mental, as the victim experienced the distinctive chime of the bell triggered by any movement, however slight. Sleeping, already complicated by the collar (and most likely some sort of binding to keep hands away from the bell), was near impossible while the bell jangled mercilessly just out of reach in front of and above the prisoner's face.

The collar was also useful when multiple prisoners were being transported, the collars could be linked together by a chain, maintaining the proximity of the prisoners, while alerting a warden if one should happen to escape. What a sight to behold, a filthy mass of squalid prisoners being led from their pens, a single brass bell ringing out distinctly from above each head in a cacophony of sound and misery that would have left John Cage green with envy.

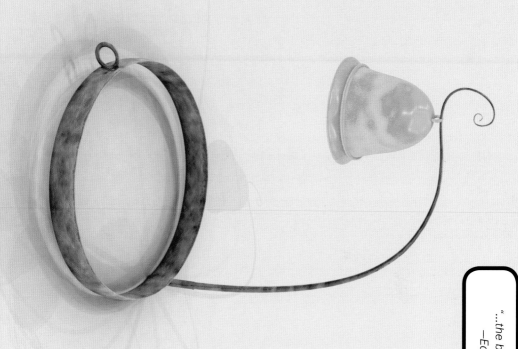

"...the bells, bells, bells, bells,/Bells, bells, bells
—Edgar Allan Poe, "The Bells"

# DUCKING STOOL

*"Of members ye tonge is worst or best,
An yll tonge oft doth breed unrest."*

Loosely translated, this means, "If you don't have anything good to say, don't say it at all." Of course, this was coming from a time when the decision of what was good or ill was decided by the men in the community. It is no wonder then that many a "temperamental" woman found herself in the ducking stool as punishment for her scolding and/or general shrewish nature. With the Ralph Kramdens of the day, it would have not been as much, "Bang! Zoom! To the moon!," as "Bang! Zoom! To the stool with ye!"

Resembling a chair more than a stool, this device was fairly common throughout all of Europe; in fact, the Domesday Book of 1084 mentions a chair belonging to the village of Chester, used to immerse scolding women in water. Its use grew from the "cucking" stool or "night chair," which was a simple stationary chair in which the scold was forced to sit for a period of time while open to public ridicule. This gradually evolved into various designs of chairs hanging from a fulcrum and beam positioned over a body of water; rivers were popular, as were cesspools, and in some cases the community well was used, which doesn't say much for the villagers' ideas of cleanliness.

Where the village did not have a fixed ducking stool, the populace made do with the portable model, looking quite like the siege weapon known as the trebuchet. Using this "treebucket," as it was sometimes called, allowed the shrew to be paraded through the town on her way to her dunking. From time to time, this humiliation would be deemed punishment enough, and the victim would be given a reprieve, undoubtedly with a warning to change her wicked ways.

*Communis rixatrix* was the legal term for "common scold"—an infraction that was punishable by the ducking stool.

*Also Known As:*
Cucking Stool
Treebucket
Night Chair

The "ducking" would unfold much as anyone would imagine—the scold forced into the chair, the chair hung over the water, and the chair levered into the water. Three dunkings seems to have been the prescribed punishment for most victims, although the elderly may have often escaped the entire dosage, as they were the ones who were in the most danger of perishing during the ritual.

Like the barrel pillory, the ducking stool would often be ornamented with scenes, a trendy one being of the scold on her way to hell in the arms of a devil. Also featured were pithy quotes, like the one above, which itself takes quite a scolding tone. The villagers' sense of irony seems not to have been well-developed.

Lest you think this a quaint contraption used in the old world hundreds of years ago, it should be noted that the last recorded ducking was in 1818 in the United States, and that the punishment was still on the books in Jersey City until 1889.[1]

1   This is not the kind of dunking that Jersey City is historically known for. That usually involved a long walk off a short pier and cement shoes.

# tHe ɢɪBBet

Travel through Europe during the Middle Ages and the gibbet, or "hanging cages" would have been an omnipresent sight, frequently displayed on the approaches to a town or near the site of a crime. Crow-picked corpses swayed in the wind, staring down upon the passersby until reduced by the elements to bits of cloth and bone. Not an "official" punishment until 1752, the justice system had at times ruled that execution was not a significant deterrent for some crimes, and reasoned that the mortification of the perpetrator's corpse would discourage all but the most hardened and ruthless criminals. After execution, the judge could decide to donate your corpse to anatomists (who had quite a difficult time obtaining bodies for dissection, but who were often obliged by resurrectionists, i.e. body snatchers, but that is another, albeit interesting, story), or to hang you from a gibbet as a warning to others. The occasional slathering in tar ensured that this curiosity would have a significant "lifetime."

The body was either hung "in chains," meaning a tight wrapping in iron bonds; or it was deposited in a slatted cage made of wood or iron. Either way, the resulting object was hung in a conspicuous location as a warning to all. The effectiveness was debatable, as one judge noted the practice was useless as a way to deter crime but an excellent way to frighten children. To be sure, the sights did frighten quite a few people in some way or another; the poet William Wordsworth was said to have fled at the sight of a gibbet. The gibbet apparently was empty, but he ran nonetheless.

In some cases, mostly having to do with piracy, the criminal was gibbeted while still alive. *Vivum excoriari*, "alive in chains," was a slow, painful death in which the lawbreaker lingered for days, starving and dehydrated. On the bright side, the executioner would not have to move the body once the victim had perished. He or she was already installed in their final resting place.

Finally, there was another unrelated device which took the name of "gibbet" —the Halifax Gibbet was an early version of the guillotine, which was less effective at cleanly separating the head from the body, but enjoyed the same infamy as its descendant, with many beggars supposedly steering clear of Halifax for fear of being gibbeted.

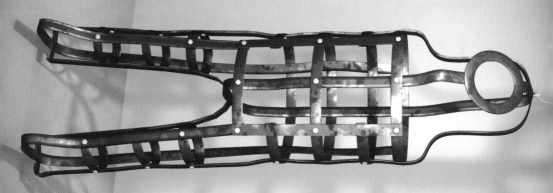

A trio of gibbets hung from the apse of the cathedral in Münster, Switzerland well into modern times.

# noisemaker's fife

Squaring nicely with Cicero's edict that the punishment should fit the crime, the noisemaker's fife and similar objects were prescribed as a tool of penance for those who had committed crimes such as disturbing the peace, foul language, "cursing in the first degree" (taking the Lord's name in vain), "revelry and din" in front of a church during services, and litigiousness.[1]

There were quite a few varieties of this device, the overarching theme being one of a musical instrument—trumpets, recorders, oboes, and fiddles were all stylish shapes. The contraption was shackled on one side around the neck, while further down the "instrument" the hands or fingers were secured by either a pillory-type lock which enclosed the wrists and held them fixed before the subject, or an adjustable clamp which closed over the fingers like thumbscrews. If there was a choice, it would be wise to choose the locking pinion over the clamp—the bar was easily tightened or loosened on the whim of whoever was in charge of securing the prisoner. Wood, brass, or iron were used in construction, and a great deal of craftsmanship went into some, as evidenced by the ornate woodworking in some of the German "Halsgeiges" or "neck violins."

As with many punitive measures, the fifes and fiddles accompanied British colonists to the Americas. Here, however, they were adapted to an all-iron construction and were used primarily for transportation and discipline of slaves, favoring the confining function over the musical instrument form.

---

1  Modern society should be thankful that this offense is not prosecuted in this way today. The courthouse would contain what looks like half a symphony orchestra.

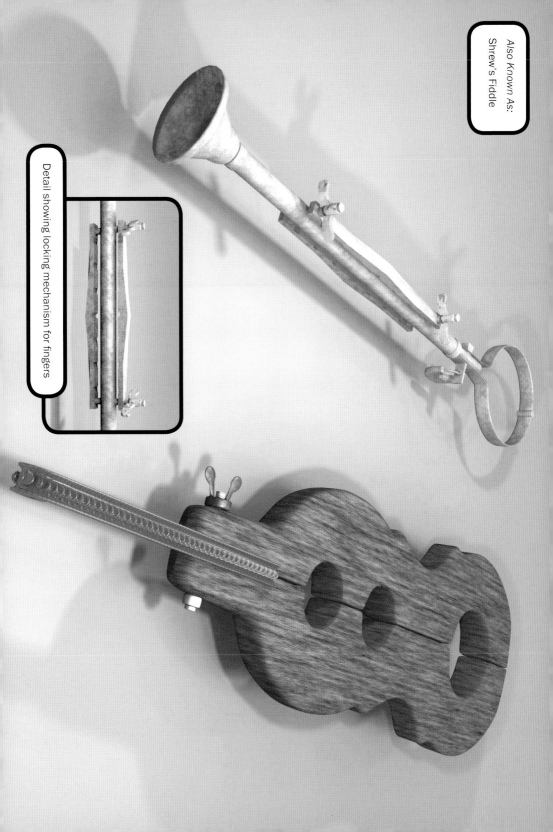

# BRANKS

*"Chester presents Walton with a bridle*
*To curb women's tongues that talk too idle"*
—Inscription on a brank, 1633, Walton-on-the-Thames

Branks were yet another way to punish the scolds of the time, and could have been seen as an escalation in the "war against the shrews." The old ducking stools and pillories, after all, allowed the prisoner to verbally harass the prosecutors between dunks and while on display. The branks not only served the stools' similar purpose of humiliating the accused, but many models also featured a way to silence the overbearing "hussy" so that there would be no chance of any back talk.

The branks appeared in Scotland in the early 1500s and their use spread quickly throughout the kingdom and subsequently all of Britain, becoming so common that some private houses in England featured an iron hook built into the side of the fireplace to accommodate the brank's chain. The man of the house, when overly nagged, simply had to send for the gaoler and he would embark on a sort-of "torture house-call," taking the brank to the homestead, locking the scold into the apparatus, and chaining it to the hook for a time period judged sufficient by the gaoler.

Branking quickly became a popular way to not only discipline scolds and shrewish women, but also as a way to punish "suspected witches," "fornicators," and "blasphemers." These latter categories opened the ranks of men to a chastisement that was formerly reserved for women, literally demonstrating that "what's good for the goose is good for the gander."[1] Witches entered the fold because

---

1  Although it is hard to imagine that there were any men demonstrating for their right to be "brankit."

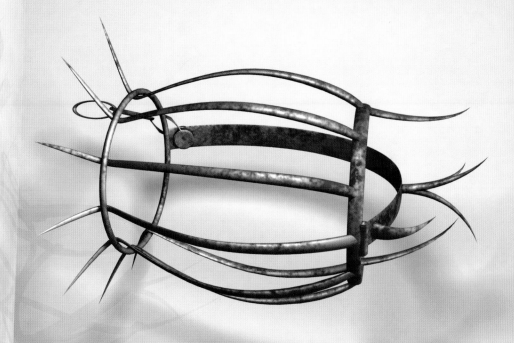

"Branks might be used with splendid effect in these degenerate days. We commend the idea to our legislators."

— from The Book of Torture and Flagellation by Richard Sair, 1944

Also Known As:
Scold's Bridle
Witch's Bridle

there was a belief that they could cast spells while on trial—the brank took care of any utterance. Fornicators were those who had fathered or borne bastard children, and the blasphemers were those who had said something critical of the clergy or church. These suffered a literal superfecta of punitive measures—"brankit, stockit, dukit and banisit."

The mechanism resembled an iron framework helmet with a lockable collar. Within the frame an iron shaft extended into the captive's mouth. This shaft acted as a gag, pressing against the tongue and making any kind of intelligible speech impossible. To further dissuade the wearer from speaking, the gagging device could be studded with short spikes or "rowelled like a spur." Any attempt at talking would lacerate the tongue and interior of the mouth, so most unfortunate captives would stand in silence.

To add insult to injury many branks were fitted with a chain for leading the offender to the town square for a good dose of public ridicule. Oftentimes a bell was fitted to the top to alert the townspeople of the approaching miscreant, resulting in most likely a stampede of citizens eager to humiliate the prisoner.

Anyone believing that torture devices were not built with a great deal of craftsmanship and ingenuity would have been disavowed of that belief after examining the many configurations of the branks. The designs range from the purely utilitarian to the fanciful, with the representation of asses and pigs dominating the latter. A village took great pride in the appearance of their brank and accordingly hired skilled blacksmiths for their construction.

Detail of the "spurs," which were inserted into the mouth.

# Piety BeLt

Instantly recognizable from a recent popular film as a smaller, concealable device, the piety or "self-mortification" belt was originally designed to be worn by those in the self-flagellation ranks of religious zealots. The idea was to take asceticism one step further and to actively seek out pain and discomfort, which would in theory allow the participant to experience a spiritual awakening.

The belt was constructed of interlocking metal loops which turned inwards like fishhooks or barbed wire, over two hundred in all. The intent was not to penetrate the flesh, but to irritate and cause great discomfort, like the hairshirts worn by penitents. However, there are claims that the belt was also used on unwilling participants as a means of torture.

An unsourced story tells of a Spanish bandit who kidnaped a French woman and locked her within a particularly sharp mortification belt. Although a bandit, he apparently drew the line at rape, hypothesizing that the pain of the belt coupled with confinement would cause her to give herself willingly to him. The anecdote does not relate why he thought that she would feel very amorous after being perforated with the tines of the belt.

In modern times, Opus Dei (a personal prelature of the Catholic Church) does in fact allow some members to wear smaller belts which are fitted around the upper thigh. They are prescribed to be worn about 2 hours per day, except on feast days. They are absolutely not meant to break the skin, but to cause irritation.

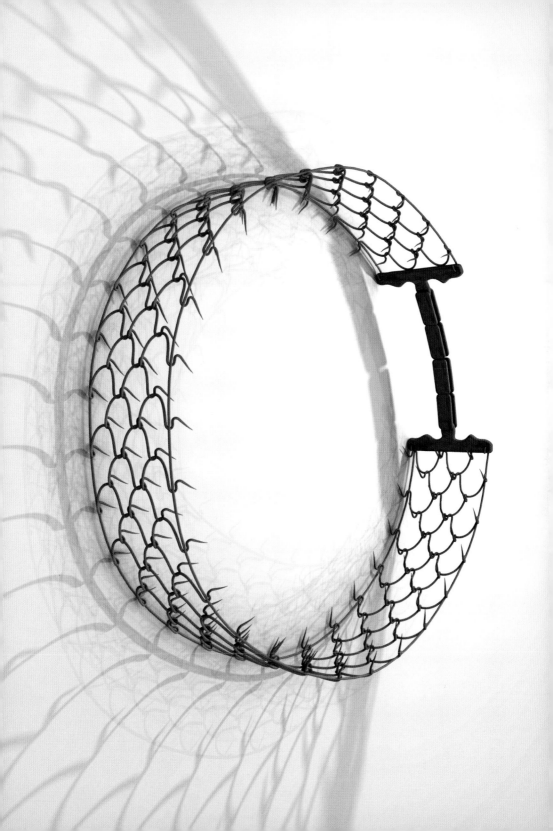

# CHAIN SCOURGE

When the punishment absolutely, positively has to leave a mark, nothing beats one of the myriad whips, flails, and scourges that have been used throughout time and throughout the world.

Whipping or flogging has long been a punishment both easy to presribe and easy to inflict, designated for such various crimes as thievery, illegitimate births (both for fathers and mothers), drunkenness, and blasphemy. In the military it was the long-standing cure-all for just about every infraction, and in just about every case, both military and civil, it was a public spectacle, with dedicated "whipping posts" where the punishment was fulfilled.

This particular example was in use in the castle of Nuremburg. It consisted of a sturdy wooden handle carved with indentations for a better grip and three chains of seven links each. The links were forged with flat, sharp edges in order to more quickly remove the flesh from the back, a feat which even a leather or rope whip could easily accomplish.

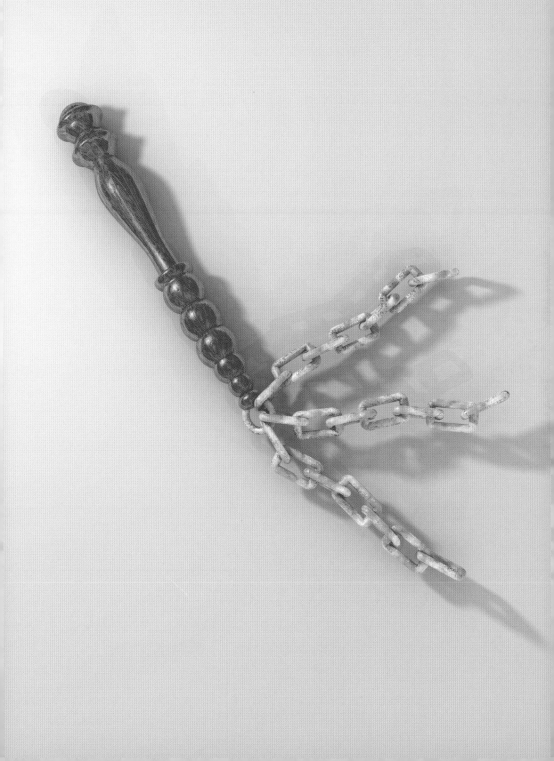

# II. CRUSHING EMBRACE

*"More weight!"*

*—Giles Corey, during his fatal pressing at the hands of the Salem Witch Trials*

# HeAD CRUSHER

The apparatus known as the head crusher has had a long history of service in the art of the torturer; the earliest mention of a device specifically built for crushing the head is in the Middle Ages, and there exists anecdotal evidence of its use up to the present day, albeit with an insert of padding so as to leave no mark upon the victim.

A versatile machine, the head crusher could be used as either an interrogation device, or if the torturer wished to "go all the way," as a method of execution. The difference, of course, lies in the amount of pressure applied. After placing the prisoner's head within the inverted bowl and resting the chin on the bottom bar (a "chinrest" which is misnamed), the inquisitor could slowly turn the top screw, closing the distance between the bowl and the bar, compressing the head in a sandwich of iron.

At early stages of compression, with the pain perhaps equal to an intense migraine, the bowl could be tapped with various force by an iron mallet in concert with the questioning—this sent reverberations of pain throughout the prisoner's skull. It was at this stage of compression, perhaps a little further along in extreme cases; that the torture ended and what was an execution began. Twisting the screw ever tighter, the head was slowly crushed like a grape in a press—the teeth, being harder than the surrounding bone, would break through the jawbones; the eyes would be forced out and forward from their sockets; and finally the skull would fracture, leaking fluid and brain matter—an execution that was decidedly messy and unconscionably cruel.

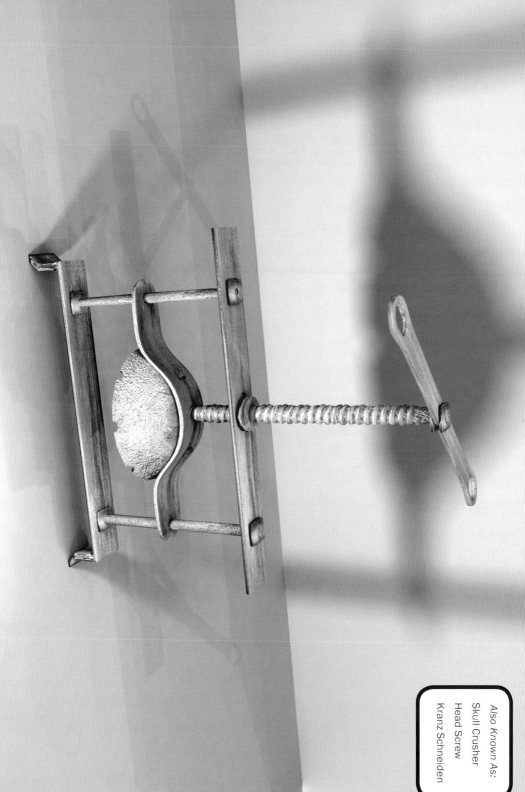

# skULL spLitteR

While the head crusher applied force to the top and bottom of the head, eventually forcing out the contents, the skull splitter squeezed the cranium from either side, with the additional tormenting feature of penetrating spikes. The design somewhat resembled the "halo" that neck injury patients must wear to immobilize the spine; a circle of iron encompassing the skull just above the browline. This device, however, was fitted snugly like a circlet, the spikes penetrating the flesh.

As with the head crusher, the skull splitter could be used as an engine of torture or of execution. A few turns of the screw and the spikes would penetrate the flesh; a few more and they would crack the bone beneath. It may have taken a masterful torturer to discern the point of no return—the point at which the spikes and pressure did irreparable damage and the victim ultimately perished. Varying degrees of softness in human skulls, whether real or imagined, would certainly have played a part in this. A single handle on the side could be jerked side to side or up and down to provide extra persuasion during an interrogation.

At the most extreme, the skull splitter was used to execute the prisoner, either by the extreme pressure which would truly "split" the skull, or by hoisting the victim into the air via the handles on the sides. The result would be the splitting and separation of the cranial cap (like a medical exhibition skeleton, sans hook and eye), or the separation of the vertebrae of the neck. Either was ultimately fatal.

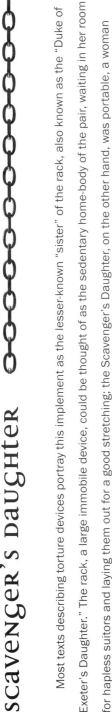

# SCAVENGER'S DAUGHTER

Most texts describing torture devices portray this implement as the lesser-known "sister" of the rack, also known as the "Duke of Exeter's Daughter." The rack, a large immobile device, could be thought of as the sedentary home-body of the pair, waiting in her room for hapless suitors and laying them out for a good stretching; the Scavenger's Daughter, on the other hand, was portable, a woman ready and willing to call on her unlucky objects of affection, crushing them in her embrace.

The name "Scavenger" is a corruption of the surname of the man who first standardized the use of this device, one Sir Leonard Skeffington (or Skevington), the Lieutenant of the Tower of London for Henry VIII. Variously known as Skeffington's Gyves, Skeffington's Iron, and Skeffington's Daughter, the machine was remarkably simple yet brutally efficient. A stout iron band hinged at one side and fitted with an adjustable lock on the other was all that was necessary. The prisoner was made to kneel with his chin on his knees, surrounded by the hoop as if he were an oaken cask. The victim was then locked into the device, crushing him into a fetal position. The standard timespan for this torture was one and a half hours.

The crushing of the body resulted in severe cramping, cracked ribs, and collapsed lungs. As time passed, blood from burst capillaries would flow from every orifice of the body, and in at least one case, from the hands and feet.

Different models of the gyves went beyond the simplicity of the single hinged band, not so much crushing the victim as confining him or her into a single position—neck, hands, and feet bound with the knees pulled towards the face. The Italian "Cicogna" or "stork" is an example of this variant. The prisoner could be kept in this device for longer stretches of time; however the result was mostly the same—cramped, cracked, and collapsed.

*gyve*—Archaic n. A shackle or fetter, especially for the leg.

Pictured is the Italian *Cicogna*.

# Knee Splitter

"Not just for knees anymore!," an advertisement might have noted, had the knee splitter a marketing blitz aimed at the discriminating torturer. It would have been correct, for this eponymous contraption was hardly reserved for use on just the knees. Any body joint that could be comfortably fit between the clamps was fair game.

A wooden clamp, not unlike a carpenter's vice, formed the basis of the apparatus. Inserted in and between either clamp were the ubiquitous sharpened iron points. Elbows, knees, ankles, or wrists were lacerated and crushed between the teeth as the screws were tightened—a crippling injury in most instances.

# foot press

Another entry in the "torture-devices-that-crush-the-extremities" line, the foot press resembles the thumbscrews, the head crusher, and the knee splitter in its mechanism and action on the body.

Resembling a typesetting press, the foot press would have been used on a victim that had been adequately restrained, usually in a heavy, immobile chair. A foot was placed between the bottom ribbed plate and the top screw—the ribbing not for traction as much as an addition to the crushing action. The top featured either a bar that crushed the foot—like the thumbscrews—or a screw which bored into the foot—an "instep borer." Crushing injuries would most likely leave the sufferer hobbled and lame, while the wounds caused by the screw rarely healed—a death sentence in the foul conditions of the time.

Also Known As:

Foot Press

Toe Breaker

Instep Borer

Malay Boot

# thUMBSCREWS

*"Oh, not so gently—another turn, another. Stop, Stop! No more!"*
*—William of Orange, trying the thumbscrews on himself*

Few torture devices are as recognizable in their simplicity as the thumbscrews, which hold the record for the number of cute-sounding nicknames. To modern ears, *"Pilniewinks"* sounds benign and dainty, perhaps the character from a cartoon. To those familiar with their clutch, however, the name belied a much different and painful reality.

Consisting in the most simple of forms as two flat pieces of wood or metal in which the fingers, thumbs or toes were crushed, the thumbscrews most likely owed their popularity and ubiquitousness to their portability and ability to create the greatest amount of pain for the least amount of work. Few people have not experienced (nor soon forget) the intense throbbing pain of crushing a digit with a hammer or in a door jamb. Imagine this pain lingering for hours, and you can appreciate the high value that the torturer placed on the thumbscrews.

A crude, wooden design of the thumbscrews ("Pyrowykes") appeared in Scotland in the late fourteenth century. From then, they were a staple of the torturer's craft, with notable refinements in design and construction added from the Russians, English and Germans. The devices often were works of art in their own right, forged by a prominent blacksmith specifically for the governing body.

Complex swirls, elaborate threads and precise engineering showcased the skill of the smith.[1] In the *Constitutio Criminalis Theresiana*, published in Vienna in 1769, there are detailed engineer's renderings of the official versions of the thumbscrew to be used during the *"peinliche Fragen"* (painful questions), complete with the precise location of pressure points.

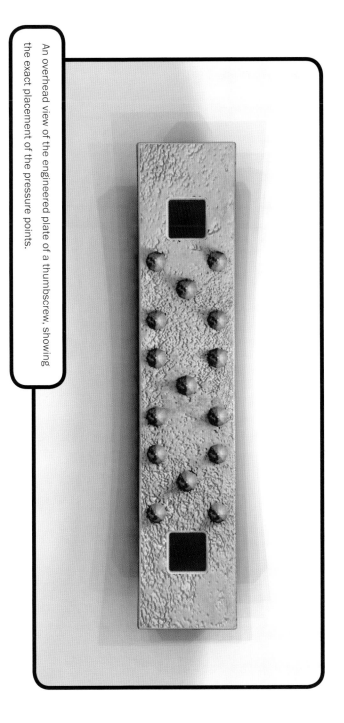

An overhead view of the engineered plate of a thumbscrew, showing the exact placement of the pressure points.

---

1 In one case, the smith who made the screw had to be called to remove them from the victim, although it is not noted whether it was the fault of his design or the over-tightening of the screws. In either case, not a favorable outcome for the victim.

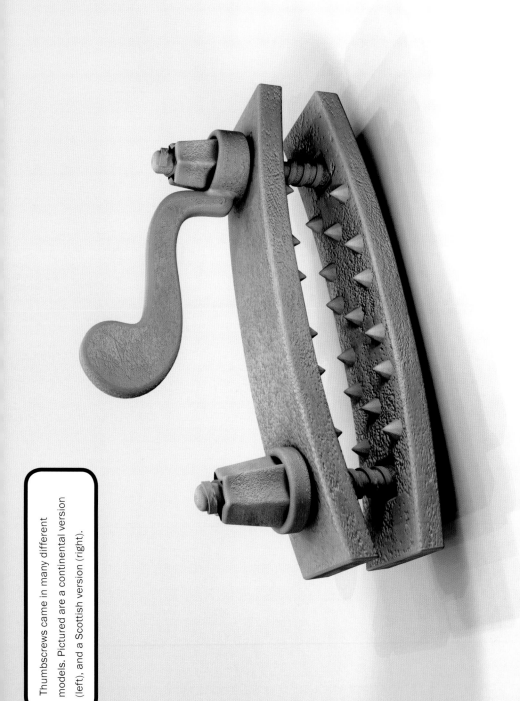

Thumbscrews came in many different models. Pictured are a continental version (left), and a Scottish version (right).

# SPANISH BOOT

The Spanish Boot works under the principle that if you force a lot of stuff into a tight solid space, something will be forced out. Something's got to give, and when iron, wood, flesh and bone are competing for the same small space, invariably it's the flesh and bone that is forced out, with painfully horrific results.

There were many variations of this device, but the end result was the crushing and mutilation of a victim's leg or legs. A Scottish version (the "bootkin") was not so much a boot as an elongated wooden box of customized length into which the legs were inserted. Strong wooden wedges were then driven by mallets between the victim's legs and the surrounding planks. A contemporary description relates that the crushing was so forceful that blood mixed with marrow "spouted forth in great abundance."

The example rendered here is a Spanish version which was popular in the torture chambers of the Inquisition. It consisted of two semicircular pieces of wood which were held together by iron bands on the ends, and an iron clamp and screws in the middle. Within the boot there were small iron knobs which served to tightly grip the unfortunate limb. Once the prisoner's leg was inserted and the clamp tightened, the inquisitor would insert wooden wedges into the boot between the leg and the walls of the device. If posed questions were not answered to the satisfaction of the inquisitors, the wedges were driven by hammer further into the boot, compressing and crushing the leg contained within, with the aforementioned results.

Of course, this version could be thought of as the Cadillac of boots (or more properly the Cadillac Seville of boots). Those inquisitors without a specially-made boot could get by with upright boards tightly bound around the legs and the same wedges, the upshot being that the entire length of leg was available for the torturer's attentions.

42

Also Known As:

Spanish Gaiter

Bootkin

Buskin

# III. fearful penetration

"Is it safe?... Is it safe?"

—Dr. Christian Szell, Nazi dentist, from the film "Marathon Man"

# INTERROGATION CHAIR

The interrogation chair was an essential piece of furniture—something an outside observer would believe was necessary for the correct "feng shui" of a torture room—from the time of the Inquisition on. Any serious torturer would have this versatile device placed in an area of distinction in his chamber, for even at its sight some prisoners would quickly change from tight-lipped mutes to the most obliging of conversationalists.

And who could blame them? One version was constructed of heavy wood with sharp iron spikes (up to 2,000) inset within the frame and covering almost every flat surface. Leather straps ensured the victim could make only small movements while fitting snugly against the keen points; stripping the prisoner bare ensured that every inch of exposed flesh could be easily pierced. Rocking the subject or striking his or her limbs could cause incredible pain, and the agony would certainly have spiraled out of control as the victim twitched away, only to cause more torment as another body part was perforated.

Another model, made of iron and used extensively during the infamous Spanish Inquisition, featured stocks made of iron for the captive's bare feet. Coal-burning braziers could be placed nearby, slowly heating the iron and burning the flesh from the legs and feet. The effect could be multiplied with the addition of lard or oil which essentially basted the outer layers of skin, the consequence of which, in one description, left the torture room quite "savoury."[1] There is little wonder that this is yet another device which bears the "Spanish" moniker.

---

1   It is hoped that "savoury" meant something entirely different during the time of the Inquisition.

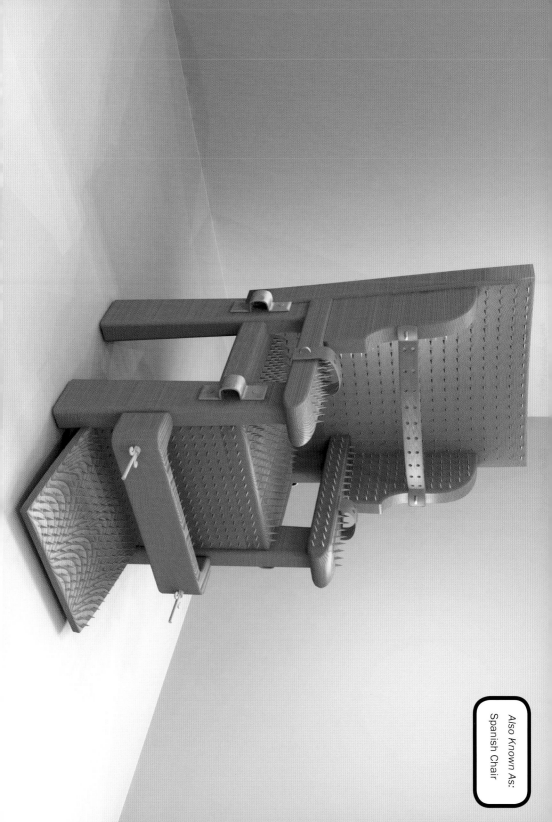

Also Known As:
Spanish Chair

Modern versions dispense with the spikes, as the torturers are usually more interested in hiding wounds than their predecessors.

A metal chair fastened to a car battery is popular, as is the "*al kursi al Almani*," or "German Chair" used in the Middle East—a frame of metal much like a lawnchair with an extensible back rest, which when tilted backwards can extend the spine to the point of breaking.

# IRON MAIDEN

"The celebrated original Iron Maiden (*Eiserne Jungfrau*)," as an illustrated catalog describes it, has a legendary yet murky history. Outnumbered only by the number of experts denying its use as an engine of torture are the number of anecdotes assuring us that it did indeed exist and was used extensively. No matter the opinions, the truth is that the maiden was a horrendous device that evoked what can only be named a visceral reaction of dread. Whether or not it was ever used on a consistent basis, the form of a woman studded with mutilating spikes is an archetype embedded in Western culture, extending as far back in time as the Greeks.

The first reference was recorded by the Greek historian Polybius, who wrote of Nabis, a ruler of Sparta. According to the historian, Nabis had built a likeness of his own wife, studded with hidden, piercing spikes. When a guest refused Nabis' requests for money, he would offer the embrace of his "wife" as a persuasion. A hidden switch in the mannequin raised the arms and extended the spikes, pinning the unlucky visitor. Presumably, the request was then granted.[1]

Jumping forward to the Spanish Inquisition, anecdotes tell of a "Virgin Mary" device almost exactly the same as the device of Nabis. In this scenario, however, the inquisitors would implore a prisoner dazed with torture to confess his sins to the Holy Virgin, prodding them closer until a mechanism in the arms sprang forward to capture the victim in an iron spiked embrace.

---

1  Presumably, the guest was also blind drunk to believe that a mannequin was a real person.

These maidens, though ambiguously documented, were ancestors of the final "Iron Maiden" form. In this incarnation (described first in a 1515 execution in Nuremberg), the maiden retained her spikes, but they were set inside what was like a cabinet or a hinged sarcophagus; the "embrace" or "kiss" was the closing of the doors upon the victim, piercing him in painful yet non-lethal areas of the body. At least one mention is made of the ability to move the spikes among different settings within the maiden, according to the punishment. Another narrative explains that after a lingering death, a trap door opened beneath the device, depositing the corpse upon a series of blades suspended above an underground stream. All sources agree that death only came after a lengthy time of suffering.

The most famous "Iron Maiden"—the *Eiserne Jungfrau*, which resided in the collection of torture instruments in the castle of Nuremberg, was destroyed in Allied bombing in 1944. A catalog of a traveling exhibition prior to the bombing lists her as item #636, and "made of strong wood, bound together with iron bands."

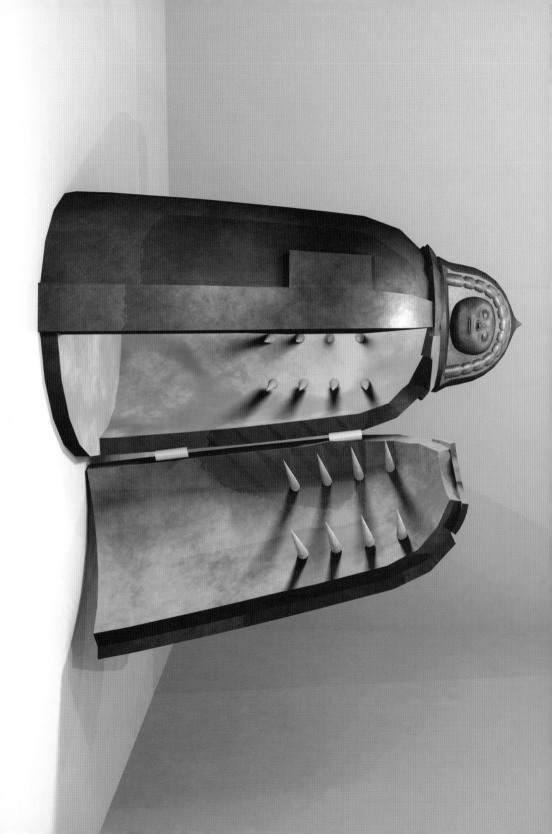

# HERETIC's fORK

Extend your chin as far back as it will go, as if you are looking straight up into the sky. Now push it back even further until the muscles in the back of your neck cramp. Now imagine that there are a total of four sharpened prongs digging into the flesh beneath the bones of your chin and sternum. Finally, imagine holding this position for hours and you can begin to envision the pain caused by the heretic's fork.

The fork was an iron device, about the span of an adult hand, with two sharpened points at each end, strapped within a short leather belt. Engraved in the side was the word, "abiuro" (I recant). Prisoners charged with the crime of heresy against the church were forced to "wear" the heretic's fork until they uttered the word.

Obstinate captives who refused to recant would be declared an "impenitent heretic" and queued up for the "auto da fé" (act of faith)—a ceremony that culminated in the heretic's death by burning at the stake. These "autos da fé" (the plural of the term) were quite a sight to behold, as the condemned heretics were led in a line to the public square, dressed in their san benitos (a yellow sack cloth garment painted with flames, dragons, and devils) and corozas (caps resembling a dunce cap—and a possible origin for the same). Throughout the proceedings priests accompanied the condemned, exhorting them to repent—as if they didn't have enough to worry about, they were on the receiving end of a large amount of guilt. The upside was that after repenting, the prisoner was strangled to death before being burned, demonstrating that no good deed ever goes unpunished.

According to the Catechism of the Catholic Church (1997), Paragraph 2089: "*Incredulity* is the neglect of revealed truth or the willful refusal to assent to it. *Heresy* is the obstinate post-baptismal denial of some truth which must be believed with divine and catholic faith, or it is likewise an obstinate doubt concerning the same. *Apostasy* is the total repudiation of the Christian faith. *Schism* is the refusal of submission to the Roman Pontiff or of communion with the members of the Church subject to him."

# st. eLmo's BeLt

St. Elmo (or Erasmus) was a bishop during the time of the Roman Emperor Diocletian, who was persecuted as a Christian. Most people are aware of the meteorological phenomenon known as "St. Elmo's fire," which was seen by sailors and interpreted as a sign of his protection. However, he is also invoked for protection against abdominal discomfort and pain, because at one time he was allegedly tortured with hot iron hooks inserted into his intestines by Diocletian's soldiers. This torment he miraculously survived.

The eponymously named belt contains inward pointing iron spikes deliberately positioned to penetrate the stomach, intestines and bowels when worn. An attached chain is used to increase the pain by forceful pulling against the belt, resulting in deeper and more extensive perforation.

# IV. the unkindest cut

*"This was the most unkindest cut of all."*

*—William Shakespeare, Julius Caesar (III, ii, 187)*

# eaR CHOPPeR

Did this exist as a device of torture? Most likely not, as it would have been just as simple to cut an ear from a head with a sharp knife; why involve such an elaborate setup as a head-encompassing iron cage with hinged blades attached? Not to mention the difficulty of adapting the solid cage into a "one-size-fits-all" capacity, taking into account the varied sizes and shapes of the human head. However, consider your head within the cage, your ears poking from the holes, with the threat of sharpened blades hanging within inches. There is a lot to be said for the threat of mutilation—a unique form of psychological torment.

Be it fact or demented imagining, it still serves as an example of a particularly bizarre torture device.

# mutiLation sHeaRs

These devices were designed solely for the ripping, tearing, shredding or cutting of exposed flesh or extremities. In form, they resembled somewhat the shears used to clip the wool from sheep, with a screw and nut combination added to the end opposite the hinge, used to apply the necessary tension to cut through the skin. Their function followed closely—the "mutilation" shears were generally used to trim fingers or toes away from the body after the bones had been crushed, while the "torture shears" were a latter steel construction used to slice pieces of flesh from the body, much like the Chinese execution method of *Leng Tch'e* (death by a thousand cuts, literally, "humiliating and slow").

It is said that some torturers were so skillful with the shears that they could make slices resembling stars and circles by bunching the flesh in particular ways before the cut was made, much like creating a snowflake from a folded piece of paper.

# mouth opener & tongue tearer

Generally reserved for "crimes of the tongue," such as heresy or blasphemy, the tongue tearer was used to destroy or completely remove the offending organ. Separating the tongue from the body, however, proved to be difficult without an efficient way to hold the mouth open while performing the procedure. That was the job of the mouth opener.

After securely binding the accused, it would have been fairly easy to force the plates of the mouth opener between the jaws, cranking the teeth apart and exposing the tongue. A quick clip of the shears would catch the squirming tongue between the blades of the tearer. Essentially a solid muscle, the tongue takes considerable force to sever—that is where the screw on the back of the tearer took over. Tightening the jaws with the screw provided the excruciatingly gradual and necessary force to cut through the root of the tongue.

St. Louis (Louis IX, King of France), ruled that blasphemers should have their tongues torn and pierced with a hot iron. Clever citizens changed their language in a sort of rhyming slang—therefore, *"Tete de Dieu!"* (God's Head!) became *"Tete bleu!"* ("Head of blue!"), *"Sang de Dieu!"* (Blood of God!) became *"Sang bleu!"* ("Blue blood!"), and *"Sacre Dieu!"* ("Holy God!") became—*"Sacre bleu!"*

# guillotine

*"They have an engine that wondrous quicke and well,*
*Sends Thieves all headless unto Heav'n or Hell."*
—John Taylor, *"Beggar's Litany"*

The machine that became notoriously associated with the bloody French Revolution actually began its life in England, made its way to Scotland via an unlucky commissioner, and was eventually adopted and improved by a French physician who, contrary to popular belief, did not perish beneath its efficient blade.

The use of the device can possibly be traced as far back as the Romans, who according to some accounts, used a similar apparatus in the martyrdom of St. Matthew. The heavy blade was not suspended over the victim's neck, however. In this case, the blade rested on the back of the neck and was struck with a heavy club or mallet until the head popped off, a considerable feat which must have taken multiple blows by a stout executioner.

The first definitive appearance of a guillotine-like device was in the West Yorkshire town of Halifax, England, during the late thirteenth century. Condemned thieves faced a machine strikingly similar to the guillotine with a flat, ax-like weighted blade suspended by a cord from a height above the criminal's neck. The other end of the cord terminated in a pin fixed in a block at the base of the gibbet. Pulling the pin from the block released the blade mechanism to travel down the grooved legs with enough force to separate the victim's head from his body. (A particular story, which must be fanciful, relates that a woman with wicker baskets happened to be passing the gibbet just as an execution was concluding. The blade struck with such force that the head bounced towards her and landed squarely in one of her baskets. Another onlooker insists that the head bounced not into her basket, but onto her apron, where it fixed itself with its teeth, hanging there like a tick.) In an early display of democratic tendencies, the crowd (or as many as could reach it) would pull the pin at the same time, so that no single person could be said to be responsible for the death of the condemned and bestowing upon him a kind of group punishment. In an early display of ironic anthropomorphism, a sheep or horse rustled by the victim would be attached to the pin. A quick slap or shoo would send the animal running, pulling the pin from its socket and dispatching its would-be captor.

The infamy bestowed upon the gibbet at Halifax was noted by the Scotsman James Douglas, the 4th Earl of Morton, who commissioned one to be built in Edinburgh in 1564. This engine was known as the "Scottish Maiden," and it was kept even busier than its older sister in Halifax, separating over 150 heads from 150 bodies in its 140 years of use. One of those so unlucky to meet his end at the embrace of the Maiden was none other than James Douglas himself, who was executed in 1581 for complicity in the murder of the Duke of Albany.

In 1789, during the early stages of the French Revolution, Dr. Antoine Louis suggested to the physician Joseph-Ignace Guillotin to investigate an efficient, mechanical and egalitarian means of execution, recommending as an example the Halifax gibbet. Guillotin promoted the idea of this machine that would be used to behead criminals quickly, painlessly, and equally, and its use was officially adopted in 1792. Dr. Louis set to work and devised a version with considerable improvements such as a hinged plank ("bascule") on which to lay the prisoner, and the "lunette" which held the head in place before the blade. The first machines were known as "Louisette" or "Louison," but the public preferred the name "Guillotine," much to the chagrin of the Guillotin family. Dr. Guillotin lived to the ripe age of 76, perishing not under the blade of his eponymous device, but of a carbuncle in his left shoulder.

From 1793–1794 in France, the guillotine worked at a rapid clip, separating anywhere from 15,000 to 40,000 heads from their bodies. It stood as the only method of execution in France, and its last use was in 1977, closed to the public, in stark contrast to the public spectacles during the Reign of Terror.

A little-known chapter of the guillotine saga is its use by the Germans during and after the Nazi regime, where it was known as the "Fallbeil" (falling axe). The Germans, perhaps taking a page from their engineering heritage, shortened the uprights and increased the weight of the blade, reducing the overall size from a machine suited to the centerpiece of a courtyard to a short, squat device not much taller than a man that could fit easily in a room. The Nazis used the guillotine to execute criminals (those who were not political prisoners), and some sources estimate that these short engines finished off more people than during the French Revolution. The final German beheading took place in West Germany in 1947.

Also *Known* As:

Halifax Gibbet

Scottish Maiden

Louisette/Louison

Fallbeil

National Razor

The Widow

People's Avenger

The Red Theatre

# V. SHEER BRUTALITY

"Brutality creates respect."

—Adolf Hitler

# tHe WHeeL

Out of all of mankind's inventions, the wheel ranks among the most revolutionary and ubiquitous, so it is no surprise that its shape found its way into the torturer's toolbox. Besides the obvious accessibility and prevalence of the wheel in medieval societies, it is possible that the shape appealed to the notion of the "wheel of fate," in which one's fortune could just as easily turn to misfortune by the turn of the wheel; a high point always having an extreme opposite low point. Many unfortunate souls ended at this low point in their fate, and perished by being "broken on the wheel."

The use of the wheel differed in its usage. The victim was either tied to the wheel laid out horizontally on the ground, its spokes serving as a frame, or the prisoner was tied directly to the ground, sprawled in the shape of an "X." In the first example, a heavy iron bar was used to systematically break the bones of the extremities, the spokes of the wheel serving to hold the limbs above the ground, thereby easing the necessary force. In the second method (and the device pictured here), the wheel was actually used as the bludgeoning device, the rim surrounded by iron bands with shovel-like protrusions. In either instance, the victim was reduced to a mass of twisted flesh, every bone of the arms and legs broken in two. The condemned that was lucky received a final "coup de grace" (literally, "blow of mercy") to the stomach that would presumably kill outright, or the "retentum"—death by strangulation. Even worse, the unlucky were "braided" into the spokes of the wheel like a pretzel, easily accomplished since the arms and legs were the consistency of limp ropes. The wheel and its passenger was hoisted vertically along the axle and left to the elements, no doubt a delicacy for the crows of the area.

Breaking on the wheel was an execution method used throughout continental Europe, but it particularly appealed to French and German executioners, who used it extensively during the eighteenth century. There were only a handful of cases in England and Scotland, where it was known as being "broken on the row." The last recorded use was by the Dutch in 1805.

The legendary St. Catherine of Alexandria is sometimes known as "St. Catherine of the Wheel," because of the story of her martyrdom. Using her saintly powers of persuasion, she managed to convert a large number of pagans to Christianity. Unfortunately, she failed to convert the most powerful, the Roman emperor, and was subsequently condemned to an execution upon the breaking wheel. The legend states that at her touch, the wheel broke into pieces. The backup method of beheading proved to be much more effective, and she was martyred for her beliefs. She was later canonized as the patron saint of wheelwrights and mechanics, ironically some of whom undoubtedly built the wheels which were used to execute other unlucky souls.

# BRAZEN BULL

*"Perilaus, roasted in the bull he made,*
*Gave the first proof of his own cruel trade."*

*—Ovid*

Perhaps the most unique of all devices used for execution, the brazen bull was a loathsomely clever Greek invention.

The story is that a brass-founder by the name of Perilaus (or Perillus) presented the tyrant Phalaris with an ingenious execution device made wholly of brass, resembling a full grown bull. Through a small door in the side or the back of the bull (the description varies), the condemned would be placed inside, enclosed by the bull's body. A raging fire was stoked beneath the center of the contraption, slowly roasting the criminal. The sounds of the prisoner's agonies were funneled up the neck of the bull, and either flute pipes or clever fluted passages concealed in the neck transformed the echoing shrieks and screams into the bellowing sounds of a lowing bull.

Perilaus did not however receive the reward from the tyrant which he believed he was due, but was instead the bull's first occupant. The reason was either that Phalaris felt that Perilaus was such a demented person that he deserved to die, that the tyrant felt insulted by Perilaus' idea that he would like such a brutal device, or simply that Phalaris displayed the fickle tendencies of such tyrants to execute their subjects on a whim, and Perilaus was the unfortunate recipient. At any rate, Phalaris convinced Perilaus to clamber inside in order to demonstrate the acoustics of the device. Once inside, Phalaris had the door locked and exclaimed, "Receive the reward of your wondrous art: let the music master be the first to play!" The fires were promptly lit and Perilaus became the victim of his own invention. In an effort to keep the device in a pristine state, he was not wholly cooked, but removed and flung from a nearby cliff, only half-baked. The story does not end there, however. It seems that what goes around comes around, and Phalaris is said to have himself perished in his own bull after being overthrown by Telemachus.

The Romans later notably used brazen bulls in their executions of early Christians, some of whom were later beatified. St. Eustace allegedly met his end in one (crammed together with his wife and sons), and in some relations of the martyrdom of St. George, he is tortured in the bull, with an addition of nails driven through the body of the device.[1]

---

1   St. George was also said to have endured these tortures: flaying with leather whips, being covered in sacks of hair, drinking poison, breaking on the wheel, being nailed to an iron bed, being forced to drink hot lead, having his head sealed inside a stone and thrown down a hill, being forced to run in red-hot iron shoes, being submerged in quicklime, being hung upside down and burned, being sawed in half, being dragged by horses, and finally beheaded. Quite a résumé for a saint.

Also Known As:
Taurus Aenus

# tHe Rack

No fictional, romanticized dungeon was ever complete without a sturdy rack deployed in the center of the room, replete with moody shadows and cloying, unmentionable stains. It was a familiar sight as well in the torture chambers of the real world, since it was an imposing engine with a purpose easily deduced by the victim. From the Greeks' judicial use all the way until the middle of the seventeenth century, the rack enjoyed a fearsome reputation throughout Europe, unmatched by just about any other device of torture.

In the simplest form, the rack was a solid wooden structure upon which the victim was stretched, arms and legs bound and pulled in opposite directions. Early versions resembled a gymnast's pommel horse, thus the equine nomenclature. A prisoner was pulled taut by ropes, his body resting on the rack between stretchings. Later improvements and refinements featured a fixed table- or ladder-like contraption that could be set either vertically or horizontally. The captive could be laid out straight or in the fashion of an "X." Yet another version, although not quite as efficient, bent the victim over the top arc of a waterwheel-like device, his or her arms and legs pulled downwards. A final improvement was the addition of a windlass at one or both ends to ease the work of the torturer.

The earliest use of torture by the rack was in the Greek judicial system. It was widely believed that a good stretching facilitated the flow of truthful information from the accused. An *Equuleus* would have been as common a sight in a courtroom as powdered wigs were centuries later, or as neck braces are today. Later, the various Inquisitions seized upon the rack as an instrument of terror, and used it extensively in the torturing of heretics, often obtaining confessions from just the act of showing the device to the accused (the "first degree"). Although not as prevalent in Britain, John Holland, the Duke of Exeter, introduced racking as a means of torture to the catalog of devices in the Tower of London. Thereafter, the punishment was known colloquially as "being married to the Duke of Exeter's Daughter" (cf. Skeffington's Daughter), and although it was not a legal form of punishment, it was used to obtain confessions, most famously from the conspirator Guy Fawkes.

As with most of the devices in this book, there were many variations and additions. The Germans added as many as three spiked rollers along the length of the horizontal frame, augmenting the agony of distension with the pain of the spikes digging into the prisoner's back. A simple yet effective Italian addition known as *"la veglia,"* (wakefulness) was a single spike under the small of the back. The victim was hard pressed to relax the tautness of his or her muscles, resulting in excruciating cramps in addition to the standard stretching.

Torture by the rack progressed through a series of degrees, which, while not an official standard, could be used as a general idea of the health and fitness of the prisoner for future torture, since much of the effectiveness of the rack depended on the simple terror of its potential use. A victim who was sure to perish after one session was of little use to the torturer, therefore it was beneficial to know the points at which the body would break beyond repair. These "degrees" should not be confused with the more general idea of first, second, and third degree torture as documented elsewhere.

The "first degree" of torture on the rack began with the victim bound, hands and feet, to stout ropes. Questions were asked, a refusal to answer effectively resulted in the gradual stretching of the entire body by increasing the tension between the ropes, in small increments. The muscles pulled taut, the most flexible part of the body, the joints, began to stretch to their limit, causing immense pain. Once the shoulders dislocated, the torturers knew they were at the limit of the first degree. The victim was removed from the rack and allowed to heal—with another racking in his or her future. This sequence of questioning, racking, and healing could be repeated many times without endangering the life of the prisoner.

The "second degree" was an order of magnitude worse than the first. The shoulders are easily dislocated compared to the joints in the knee, hips, and elbows. Unfortunately, this is exactly what happened—dislocation of the remaining flexible joints; pulled asunder from their sockets. After surviving a racking of this intensity, the victim would in all probability be permanently maimed.

In the third and final degree of racking, the last and least flexible joints in the body (those between the vertebrae), are separated. Such a trauma results in paralysis and death follows shortly thereafter. An extreme expansion such as this would result in the victim ending up quite a bit taller than he or she was originally, with one torturer claiming that one prisoner ended up an entire foot taller.

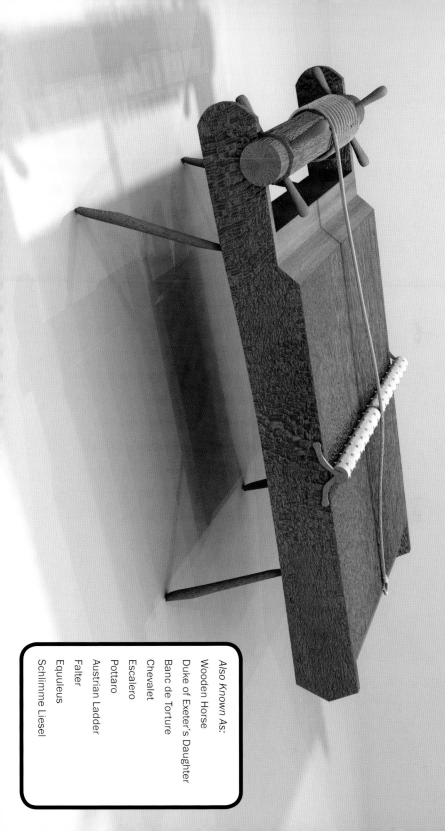

Also Known As:
Wooden Horse
Duke of Exeter's Daughter
Banc de Torture
Chevalet
Escalero
Pottaro
Austrian Ladder
Falter
Equuleus
Schlimme Liesel

# JUDAS CRADLE

A fiendishly simple device, the judas cradle was a torment that Christians of the time may have wished upon it's namesake, the betrayer of Christ. It accomplished its cruel task by taking advantage of the fact that among all parts of the human body, the nether regions are perhaps the most sensitive to pain. By applying either constant or quick, sharp pressure, even the most hardy could be broken.

The victim, bound arms and legs, was hoisted above the apex of a wooden pyramid. From this point, using a series of pulleys, the tormentor could raise or lower the prisoner onto the point, the target being all the most delicate areas—the rectum, the vagina, beneath the scrotum,[1] or on the coccyx (popularly known as the tailbone). From this point, the amount of pain followed the whim of the torturer. Strategies included bouncing the victim upon the point, dropping the victim from a height onto the point, and leaving the victim with his or her entire weight balanced on the single pressure point to face a long and agonizing night.

---

1 Known as the "taint" in the modern vernacular.

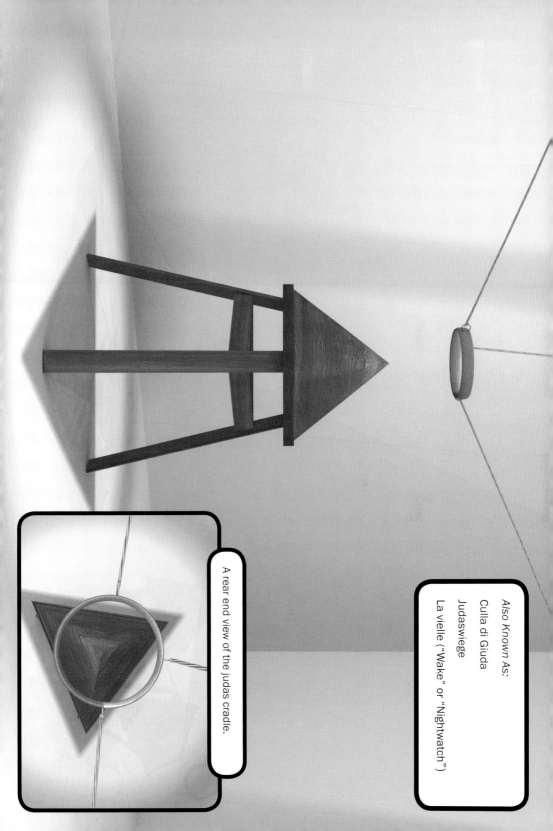

A rear end view of the judas cradle.

Also *Known As:*

Culla di Giuda

Judaswiege

La vielle ("Wake" or "Nightwatch")

# SPANISH DONKEY

Suspending a person so that he or she straddles an uncomfortable plank of wood or wedge of stone was a popular punishment in villages throughout Europe and the colonies, in fact continuing well into the American Civil War, with miscreants being paraded to the edge of the town astride a length of wood; in other words, "run out of town on a rail," in Europe, "riding the stang."

Of course, there were various configurations, the simplest being the straight rail on which the victim was displayed for the onlooker's ridicule. As the punishment progressed, the discomfort was transformed into pain, with the addition of weights for the legs, or in some cases, spikes along the edge between the condemned's legs. A seventeenth century English version, dubbed the "liar rack," featured a pentagonal cylinder on which the victim rode; the cylinder was then slowly turned beneath him or her. Weights could then be added to both the legs and arms, in order to multiply the pain.

The Spanish version, as shown here, was used by the Inquisition. The victim was stripped bare and forced to straddle the sharpened wooden edge. As the torture progressed, heavier weights were slipped around both legs, increasing the overall weight of the body atop the wedge. There are claims that in extreme cases, the wedge eventually cut through into the body cavity. Of course, this would result in an unpleasant and messy death.

# GaRRote

For an execution device which could be thought of as a hanging that requires the executioner, not gravity, to do all the work, the garrote (or "garrotte," or even "garrotte") was used extensively to cut short the lives of all manner of heretics, apostates, and murderers. Its popularity grew during the misdeeds of the Spanish Inquisition, and it was in fact the official method of civilian execution in Spain up until the latter half of the twentieth century. Old habits, it seems, die hard.

In its earliest form, the garrote involved the assembly of a rope, a sturdy post, a stout club or cudgel, and the condemned. The condemned was bound to the post, facing outwards. The rope was slipped around both the neck and the post, and the cudgel was used to twist the rope like a tourniquet, slowly compressing the windpipe and strangling the victim. It is from this cudgel or "stick" (which is what "garrote" means in Spanish) that the device is named.

Improvements featured a straight board for the victim to be seated upon (this was presumably not for the victim's comfort, but rather to make the executioner's work easier as there was more surface area on which to bind the victim and it was easier to turn the garrote at waist level), and a strap of leather or iron to replace the rope. Another refinement (pictured here), added an iron spike or razor on a screw attached to the garrote. In this version, the strap merely held the neck in place while the spike or razor crushed, penetrated, and eventually severed the spinal cord below the skull; this method was substantially more painful and was used at times when the execution of a subject called for a preceding session of torture.

Detail showing the spike which was intended to sever the spinal cord.

The garrote was used as the "merciful" means of execution by the Inquisition—heretics, unbelievers, and apostates who agreed to die as Catholics were garroted first and then burned, while the unrepentant were burned alive. Atalhuapa, the last emperor of the Incas, experienced this firsthand, after being condemned to death by burning in a mock trial set up by the Spanish conquistador Pizarro. Told by the Catholic priests that they would be lenient if he would only convert to Christianity, he agreed to a baptism and a Christian name. Juan Santos Atahualpa was then promptly garroted.

# pear of anguish ⊂○⊃○⊂○⊃○⊂○⊃○⊂○⊃○⊂○⊃○⊂○⊃○

A subject of much controversy, the pear of anguish has never been definitively proven to have been used as a torture device. However, working examples do exist and have been exhibited in different collections. Whether the pear was actually used to cause the tremendous pain with which it is associated, or whether it is just the stuff of legend—part of a gothic horror story, may never be known— but the mythology surrounding it bears relating.

The device is constructed of four metal leaves surrounding a central screw, looking much like a pear. Turning the screw causes the leaves to slowly open, expanding the circumference of the contraption. Extra protuberances may have been attached to the leaves, further increasing the size and effectiveness of the device. In use, the pear would have been inserted into the mouth, rectum or the vagina (basically any orifice in the body), and slowly enlarged. The mutilation of the throat, intestines, or cervix, respectively, generally followed.

Some sources relate that the pear was used mainly as a way to silence the prisoner, presumably to silence speech, as screaming would still be possible. These pears were supposedly "spring-loaded," springing apart at a touch, distending the mouth.

Most sources are in agreement that as a tool of torture, the manner in which the pear was used was wholly dependent on the crime. Heretical preachers or "unorthodox" laymen received it orally; with passive male homosexuals, on the other hand, the pear was forced into the rectum, while women found guilty of "sexual congress with Satan" had the most unfortunate fate of the pear being expanded within their vagina. The pears reserved for this last torment were of a larger size, it is unfairly noted.

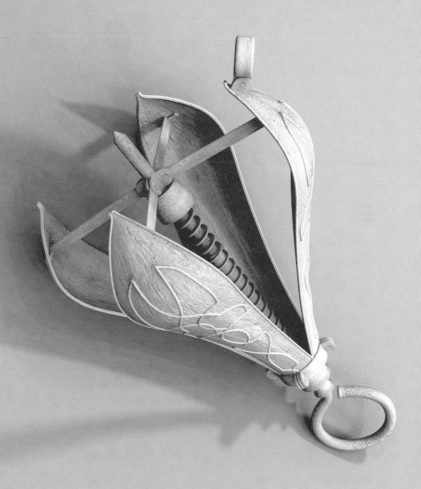

# BIBLIOGRAPHY

Abbott, Geoffrey. *The Book of Execution*. London: Headline Book Publishing, 1995.

————. *Rack, Rope and Red-Hot Pincers*. London: Headline Book Publishing, 1993.

Adams, Norman. *Scotland's Chronicles of Blood*. London: Robert Hale Limited, 1996.

Farrington, Karen. *Dark Justice*. New York: Reid International Books Limited, 1996.

Held, Robert. *Inquisition: A Bilingual Guide to the Exhibition of Torture Instruments from the Middle Ages to the Industrial Era*. Florence, Italy: Qua d'Arno, 1985.

Ichenhäuser, Julius D. *Collection of Torture Instruments from the Royal Castle of Nuremburg*. New York: J.J. Little & Co., 1893.

Innes, Brian. *The History of Torture*. London: Brown Packaging Books, 1998.

Kellaway, Jean. *The History of Torture and Execution*. New York: Lyons Press, 2000.

Kerrigan, Michael. *The Instruments of Torture*. New York: Lyons Press, 2001.

Mannix, Daniel P. *The History of Torture*. New York: Dell Publishing, 1964.

Parry, L. A. *The History of Torture in England*. New Jersey: Patterson Smith, 1975.

Sair, Richard P. *The Book of Torture and Executions*. Toronto, Canada: Golden Books of America, 1944.

Scott, George Ryley. *A History of Torture*. London: Senate, 1995.

Villeneuve, Roland. *Le Musée des Supplices*. Paris: Claude Offenstadt, 1968.